First edition for the United States
and Canada published in 2014
by Barron's Educational Series, Inc.

First published in 2014 by Wayland
Text copyright © Pat Thomas 2014
Illustrations copyright © Wayland 2014

Wayland is a division of Hachette Children's Books,
a Hachette UK company.
www.hachette.co.uk

Concept design: Kate Buxton
Series design: Paul Cherrill for Basement68
Editor: Victoria Brooker

All inquiries should be addressed to:
Barron's Educational Series, Inc.
250 Wireless Boulevard
Hauppauge, New York 11788
www.barronseduc.com

ISBN: 978-1-4380-0472-3

Library of Congress Control Number: 2013957083

Date of manufacture: May 2014
Manufactured by: WKT Co. Ltd., Guangdong, China

Printed in China

9 8 7 6 5 4 3 2 1

I Am Feeling Bashful

A FIRST LOOK AT SHYNESS

PAT THOMAS
ILLUSTRATED BY CLAIRE KEAY

BARRON'S

Do you ever feel shy?

Everyone has that feeling at some time in
their lives – even grown-ups!

Shyness is a feeling – it's kind of like being scared and worried all at the same time.

When you are feeling shy, it's easy
to think that nobody likes you or cares
about you, or wants to make friends
with you – even though that's not true.

When you are feeling shy, you worry a lot about what others think of you, and it can be hard to join in with groups or just talk or laugh with the people around you.

What about you?

Are you sometimes shy?

What sort of things do you worry about?

Feeling shy can tie your tummy up in knots and make you feel afraid of new places and people.

And it can make you want to hide away and be on your own.

Sometimes it can be nice to just play
on your own and not have to talk to
anyone or share your things.

But being on your own all the time can also
make you feel lonely and left out.

And some things are just more fun when
there are two or more of you together.

Sometimes feeling shy can even be a good thing. Shy people often think twice before doing something.

That can help keep you out of trouble!

But when you are feeling really worried, talking to your parents or teachers about how you feel is a good way to help you feel safer and more confident.

They probably all have stories about times when they felt shy…and of how things worked out much better than they thought when they tried anyway.

What about you?

Have you ever talked to a grown-up you know about when they felt shy? Try asking someone now.

When you see other people who seem
brave or who seem to always be the center
of attention, you may think they are very
different from you.

But everyone has things they are afraid of and things that make them feel shy.

You probably have lots of good ideas about fun things you'd like to do and people you'd like to meet...

...if only you weren't feeling so shy.

What about you?

What sort of things would you like to do if you didn't feel too shy?

As you get older it will be easier to let go of some of your shy feelings. And there's things you can practice now to help that happen, like saying hello to people and smiling at them – even if you don't know them well.

You could offer help to someone who needs it or try being friendly to another person who is also feeling shy.

And every once in a while – make an effort to try something new.

And when you find yourself
worrying about what others are
thinking of you…

Try to remember this
secret: most of the time
they are wondering
what you are thinking
of them!

When someone you know is shy, you can help them a lot by being kind and patient. That's because people who are shy are a little like the stars in the sky.

Sometimes you have to wait
a little while before you can
really see them shine.

HOW TO USE THIS BOOK

This book is written largely from the child's perspective. It is meant to be read with your child, or with a group of children, in a way that allows the child to open up about what he or she thinks and feels.

Everyone is different. If you're the parent of a shy child, it can be hard to watch your child struggle with shyness, especially if you were outgoing as a child. But all children, like all adults, are different. The first step is to respect that difference without judging it. Children feel shy for a variety of reasons and may feel more or less so in different situations. In some situations shyness may even be a legitimate response.

Reject labels. When you label a child as "shy" it can become a self-fulfilling prophesy or provide a wall for that child to hide behind. Get to the root of the problem. Shy behavior is often linked to feelings of embarrassment, worry, fear, or lack of confidence. Many of these feelings are developmentally appropriate and, since children all develop at different speeds, addressing the underlying feelings rather than pushing your child to do something they are not ready to do is the most effective approach.

Build emotional resilience. Shyness can be a way of not dealing with much stronger emotions such as worry or fear. Help your child to manage emotions in a healthy way, to know that there are no "wrong" feelings and that feelings like hurt or embarrassment don't last forever.

Make your child a partner in the process. Ask your child what he or she needs and think about ways that might help them overcome their shyness. Allow them time to grapple with the question rather than finding ways to "fix" things yourself. Work with your child to set small achievable goals – saying hello to someone new today or asking a question in class this week. Praise this behavior when you see it. You could even track it on a chart at home with colorful stickers to mark each milestone.

Think small steps. If your child is very shy don't expect that to change overnight. Confidence building is a process. Praise the little successes, actively seek to identify and praise your child's strengths in other areas, and don't focus too much on the times when your child slips back into shy behavior.

Set an example. Children learn by example, so talk to your child about times when you felt shy and what you did about it and who or what helped you. Stress the benefits of being more outgoing – i.e., making more friends, enjoying school more, having more fun, learning new things.

Encourage hobbies. Help your child develop passions and hobbies that they can feel completely absorbed in. Being good at something helps build confidence, and being absorbed in something means the child has less time to feel fearful or under confident.

Teachers can help by being thoughtful about group situations. Putting a shy child in a group that is loud and competitive may be counterproductive. Pairing a shy child with another shy child could help bring out the best in both.

Talking about shyness and lack of confidence is an important part of teaching about personal development and mutual understanding. In group work ask children if they have ever had times when they felt shy and what they did to overcome that feeling. Engage children in dialogue about what they can do to help shy children feel more confident, for instance being more friendly and encouraging, or asking a shy person to join in games, not teasing them if they aren't as competent as other children.

Act it out. Role-play can be a good way to help children "practice" social skills. Get the class involved in short plays about feeling shy, with each group providing an alternative ending, or use puppets to act out a story about shyness.

BOOKS TO READ

For children

Buster the Very Shy Dog
Lisze Bechtold
(Houghton Mifflin, 2001)

Halibut Jackson
David Lucas
(Andersen Press, 2005)

I'm Feeling Shy
Lisa Regan and Christiane Engel
(A&C Black, 2012)

Little Mouse's Big Book of Fears
Emily Gravett
(Macmillan Children's Books, 2008)

Let's Talk About Being Shy
Joy Berry
(Joy Berry Books, 2010)

Shaun the Shy Shark
Neil Griffiths
(Red Robin Books, 2008)

Sophie Shyosaurus (Dinosaurs Have Feelings, Too)
Brian Moses
(Wayland, 2013)

The Great Big Book of Feelings
Mary Hoffman and Ros Asquith
(Frances Lincoln Children's Books, 2013)

RESOURCES FOR ADULTS

Emotional Intelligence
Daniel Goleman
(Bantam, 1995)

Shyness – How Normal Behavior Became a Sickness
Christopher Lane (Yale University Press, 2009)

RESOURCES FOR PARENTS

www.shykids.com
A website for kids, parents, and teachers that explores what shyness is, what it feels like, and strategies to overcome it.

www.shakeyourshyness.com
Tips for dealing with shyness from clinical psychologist Renée Gilbert, Ph.D.

Helping Young Children Overcome Shyness
Web resource for parents and teachers hosted by the University of New England, featuring work by John Malouff, Ph.D., J.D.
http://www.une.edu.au/about-une/academic-schools/school-of-behavioural-cognitive-and-social-sciences/news-and-events/community-activity/psychology-community-activities/helping-young-children-overcome-shyness